# A HORRID FACTBOOK

# HORRID HENRY'S KINGS AND QUEENS

## Francesca Simon

### Illustrated by Tony Ross

Orion
Children's Books

First published in Great Britain in 2013
by Orion Children's Books
a division of the Orion Publishing Group Ltd
Orion House
5 Upper Saint Martin's Lane
London WC2H 9EA
An Hachette UK Company

1 3 5 7 9 10 8 6 4 2

Text © Francesca Simon 2013
Illustrations © Tony Ross 2013

Facts compiled by Sally Byford.

The Orion Publishing Group's policy is to use papers that are natural, renewable
and recyclable products and made from wood grown in sustainable forests.
The logging and manufacturing processes are expected to conform to the
environmental regulations of the country of origin.

ISBN 978 1 4440 0631 5

A catalogue record for this book is available from the British Library.

Printed in Great Britain by
Clays Ltd, St Ives plc

www.orionbooks.co.uk

www.horridhenry.co.uk

# CONTENTS

# Hello from Henry

**Hi gang!**

**As you know, I'm growing up to be King Henry the Horrible, when all my enemies will be flung into snake pits or catapulted over my battlements, wormy worm brothers will be in prison and homework banned on pain of death.**

But everyone, even the Lord High Ruler of the Purple Hand, can use a few handy hints about ruling the world. And boy, does this book provide them! My enemies better beware – this book is chock-full of how Kings and Queens dealt with anyone they didn't like. Take old King Murad of Turkey – he got so annoyed with some noisy ladies he had them drowned! Wow. Or Charles 1st shoving nobles who wouldn't give him extra tax money into prison. Way to go, Charles. I like your style.

Enjoy reading my spine-tingling guidebook to ruling the world.

Henry

PS – Dates are how long the king or queen reigned!

# CURIOUS
# KINGS

**Louis XIV** of France (1643-1715) had 5,000 servants who each had a special duty, like **mopping the king's brow** or **helping him to shave.**

**King Henry the Horrible would have 6,000.**

**King John** of England (1199-1216) employed a **Royal Head Holder** to help prevent his **seasickness.** Whenever he went to sea, his servant went as well, to hold King John's head steady.

**Alfonso XIII** of Spain (1886-1931) was **so deaf** he couldn't tell when the Spanish national anthem was playing. He had to have a **special servant** to tell him when to stand.

**Edward II** of England (1307–1327) enjoyed **hard work** – he liked bricklaying, roofing houses and digging holes.

**Emperor Elagabulus** of Rome (218–222) enjoyed **embarrassing** his dinner guests by putting an old-fashioned sort of **whoopee cushion** on their seats.

**Now THAT'S my kind of emperor.**

**David II** of Scotland (1329–1371) was only **three** when his mother died, **four** when he was married and **five** when he became king. During his wedding, **he wet his pants**.

**Charles II** of England (1660–1685) rubbed the dust from **Egyptian mummies** into his body because he thought it would make him as **great** as they were.

**King Afonso VI** of Portugal (1656–1683) often wore **seven coats** all at the same time, and **three or four hats** perched one on top of the other.

**James IV** of Scotland (1488–1513) liked conducting **scientific experiments**. He once sent two babies to live with a woman who couldn't speak, to see if they would make up their own language. Funnily enough, they never learned to speak at all.

**Henry III** of England (1216–1272) had the **first ever zoo** in the **Tower of London** – it included **three leopards** and a **polar bear**, which was kept on a long chain so it could swim and catch fish in the River Thames.

**King Pepi II** of Egypt (2278–2184 BC) kept flies away by having **slaves smeared in honey** close by to attract all the insects.

**Hmm. I'll remember this when I'm king.**

During the tenth century, the **Grand Vizier** of Persia, who loved reading, took all his **117,000 books** on his travels, carried on the backs of camels.

**George V** of England (1910–1936) kept the **hundreds of clocks** at the palace thirty minutes fast so that he would never be late for an appointment.

# QUIRKY
# QUEENS

**Queen Cleopatra VII** of Egypt (51–30 BC) sneaked into a palace to see Julius Caesar by ordering her soldiers to **roll her up in a carpet** and carry her inside.

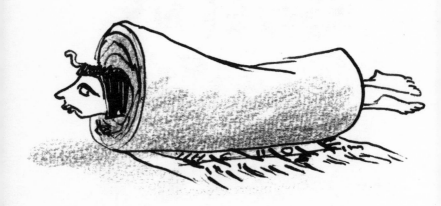

Fifteen-year-old **Lady Jane Grey** fainted when she was told she would be queen after Edward VI of England died in 1553.

When she was old and living in the countryside, **Queen Alexandra**, Edward VII's wife, liked to ride through the fields in her carriage, nodding and waving to **the cows**.

**Eleanor**, wife of Henry III of England (1216-1272), was unpopular with Londoners. But when people threw **lumps of mud** at her, Eleanor picked up the mud and threw it right back!

**Mary II** of England (1689-1694) was **mad** about animals. She had little red velvet beds made for her dogs and hung bird cages at her bedroom windows.

**Queen Marie Antoinette** of France (1774-1792) liked **pretending to be poor**. She had a **small village** with a pond built especially for her where she dressed up as a **milkmaid** and milked cows.

**Mary Queen of Scots** (1542-1567) loved playing a game called **billiards**. She even played in prison awaiting her **execution**.

**Queen Elizabeth I** of England (1558–1603) got a disease called **smallpox** which left her with scars and made her lose most of her hair. After that she covered her face with **white make-up** and wore a **wig**.

**Elizabeth I** lived until the age of **70**, but artists were **never** allowed to paint her looking old. She wanted everyone to think she was **young** and **beautiful**.

**King\* Christina** of Sweden (1632-1654) was **scared of fleas**. She had a tiny cannon made for her, so that she could fire miniature cannonballs at them.

\* **Funny fact - all Swedish monarchs were given the title of King, even the ladies.**

**Queen Victoria** of England (1837-1901) **hated children** – but she still had nine of them!

# INSIDE
# INFO

Until the **twentieth century**, nearly every country in the world was ruled by a **king** or **queen**.

But after a while, **people got fed up** of being ruled by kings and queens so now lots of countries have **presidents, prime ministers** or **dictators** instead.

Today, out of almost **200 countries**, there are only around **30** that still have a king or queen.

A king or queen who is completely in charge of a country is called an **absolute** monarch. King Henry the Horrible would definitely want to be this kind of king!

**He'd also like to be emperor of the universe.**

When there is both a **king or queen AND** a **government**, the monarchy is called **constitutional**. A constitutional king or queen represents their country, but doesn't have much power.

The title of king or queen is usually **hereditary**, meaning it passes from parent to child, with the oldest son being the 'heir' to the Crown. So if Horrid Henry's family were **royalty**, Henry would be the heir.

**Peter would be the spare. Very spare.**

Kings were once expected to lead their armies into **battle**, so it's tradition for the Crown to pass to a **son** rather than a **daughter** (because girls aren't supposed to be good at fighting!).

**George II** (1727–1760) was the **last British king** to lead an army into battle, but today the Crown still passes to the oldest son. So if Queen Elizabeth II had a younger brother, there would be a **King of England** today, instead of a queen.

If there **aren't any children**, the Crown passes to the king or queen's younger brother instead. When there isn't an obvious heir, it can all get a bit **hairy**.

When **King Charles IV** of France (1322-1328) died, both his cousin and his nephew thought they should be king, and this started a war that went on for a hundred years – known, funnily enough, as **the Hundred Years War**.

**King Henry VIII** of England (1509–1547) was so desperate for a **son** and **heir** that he got rid of his first two wives when they failed to give him a boy.

A king or queen can rule until he or she dies, which is why so many monarchs in the past have been **murdered horribly** by their enemies.

# FOUL
# FACTS

**Queen Elizabeth I** of England (1558–1603) had a very **sweet tooth**. She ate so much sugar her teeth rotted away and turned **black**!

… And she only had **four baths a year**.

**King Louis XIV** of France (1643–1715) hated washing even more than Elizabeth I did. He only took **three baths** in his whole life.

**George IV** of England (1820–1830) was **so fat** when he died, he almost didn't fit into his coffin.

**Henry IV** of England (1399–1413) had his hair cut very short so it wouldn't get infested with **head lice**.

**Vitellius**, Emperor of Rome (April–Dec 69 BC) ate **four huge meals** every day. He could eat **1,000** oysters in one go. He used to visit the **'vomitorium'** to be sick so that he could carry on eating.

**Edward VII** (1901–1910) had a horrid sense of humour. As a joke, he once left a surprise in his friend's bed – it was a **dead seagull.**

After **Charles I** was beheaded in 1649, a nobleman took one of the **king's neck bones** and used it on his dinner table to keep salt in.

When **John** became **King of England** in 1199, he gave a Christmas party where he and his guests feasted on **400 oxen, 1,000 chickens** and **1,000 eels**.

When he was young, **King Henry VIII** of England (1509-1547) had a slim **86cm** waist, but by the time he died in 1547 his waist had expanded to **152cm**. That's **nearly double**!

**King James I** of England (1603-1625) had such a **big tongue** that he **dribbled** when he ate.

**Queen Anne** of England (1702–1707) was so fat when she died that her coffin was **almost square**.

**Henry V** of England (1413–1422) was killed in battle in France, but buried in England. To avoid spreading diseases he'd picked up in France, his body **was boiled** until the **flesh** came off his **bones**, then his bones were packed into a box and shipped off home. Yuck!

# NIFTY
# NICKNAMES

**Louis XI of France** (1461–1483) was nicknamed **the Spider** because he was very clever and cunning.

**Harald I of Denmark** (958–986) was nicknamed **Bluetooth**. But he didn't have a blue tooth – it comes from an old Danish word meaning that Harald was dark-skinned and a great man.

Harald's son, **Sven I** (986–1014) was nicknamed **Forkbeard** because he had a pitchfork-style moustache.

**Queen Juana of Castile** (1504–1555) was known as **Joan the Mad** because of her bad moods and tantrums.

**Just like Moody Margaret.**

**King Richard I of England** (1189–1199) was known as the **Lionheart** because of his bravery.

His younger brother, **King John of England** (1199–1216) was nicknamed **Lackland** because he was the youngest son of Henry II and would not inherit any land.

**King Edward I of England** (1272-1307) was known as **Longshanks** because of his long legs.

**Louis VI of France** (1108-1137) was called **the Wide-awake** and **the Bruiser**, but in later life he became known as **Louis the Fat**.

When fat **George IV** (1820–1830) was still the **Prince of Wales** (which is the title given to the heir to the throne) a cheeky poet wrote a poem calling him the **"Prince of Whales"**.

**Louis X of France** (1314–1316) was known as the **Quarrelsome**, the **Headstrong** or the **Stubborn**. He liked to get his own way!

**Mary I of England and Ireland** (1553-1558) was known as **Bloody Mary** by her enemies because she had over **280** people **burned** at the stake during her five-year reign.

**Isabella**, the French wife of King Edward II of England (1307-1327) was often called the **She-Wolf of France** because many people believed that she had arranged for her husband to be **murdered**.

# TERRIBLE
# TYRANTS

**Henry VIII** of England (1509–1547) was so desperate to have a son that he got through not **one**, not **two**, but **SIX wives** – Catherine of Aragon, Anne Boleyn, Jane Seymour, Anne of Cleves, Catherine Howard and Catherine Parr.

**King Murad IV** of Turkey (1623–1640) once got so annoyed by a group of noisy ladies who were enjoying a **picnic** that he ordered his soldiers to **drown them all**.

**King Gustav I** of Sweden (1523–1560) **hacked** the royal goldsmith to **death** because he took a day off work without asking.

**Yikes!**

When **Ivan the Terrible** of Russia (1533–1584) fell out with the Archbishop of Novgorod, he had the archbishop **sewn into a bearskin** and hunted down by dogs.

**Queen Ranavalona I** of Madagascar (1828–1861) **executed** over a third of her people during her reign – by **boiling them** in water and throwing them off cliffs.

Queen Ranavalona also ordered her soldiers to **spear** Prince Rakobote, the real heir to the throne, to **death**.

**Emperor Caligula** of Rome (37–41) fed criminals to **the lions** because it was cheaper than feeding them **raw meat.**

**Emperor Elagabulus** of Rome (218–222) released **lions** and **leopards** at a **dinner party** and laughed as his guests ran **screaming** from the palace.

When **Charles I** of England (1625-1649) raised his income from £600,000 to £900,000 a year, he forced **nobles** and **knights** to pay him more **taxes**. If they refused, he **threw them into prison**.

**Peter the Great** of Russia (1682-1696) hated **beards** so much that he would rip a beard out by the roots if he saw anyone with one. But he liked **moustaches**.

**Mahomet IV** of Turkey (1648–1687) had a servant to **write his diary**. One day, when the servant couldn't think of anything to write, Mahomet **stabbed him** so that he'd have something to write about.

# PERFECT
# PALACES

**Queen Elizabeth II** of England has **nine royal thrones** – one at the House of Lords, two at Westminster Abbey, and six in the throne room at Buckingham Palace.

**Louis XIV** of France had **413** beds in the Palace of Versailles. That's a **different bed** for every night of the year – and more!

**Neuschwanstein Castle** in Bavaria, Germany, built for **King Ludwig II** in 1869, was the inspiration for the castle in Disney's *Sleeping Beauty*, and was also Baron Bomburst's Castle in the film, *Chitty Chitty Bang Bang*.

Today, **Queen Elizabeth II** of England invites around **8,000** guests to her four Royal Garden parties each year and they drink **27,000** cups of tea and eat **20,000** slices of cake. There's a lot of **washing up** afterwards!

The **Sultan of Brunei's** palace cost £300 million to build. It has **1,788 rooms** and **257 toilets**.

**Yeah, but how many TVs???**

**Emperor Shah Jehan** of India (1628–1658) built the **Taj Mahal** in memory of his wife. It is one of the **New Seven Wonders of the World**.

Low-ranking servants at **Hampton Court Palace** used to share a **toilet**, which could seat **14 people at a time** and emptied into the River Thames.

When Istanbul's **Dolmabahce Palace** was built in 1856, fourteen tonnes of **gold** were used – the same weight as **five elephants**. That's a lot of gold!

**Buckingham Palace** in London has a
**ballroom**, a cinema and a **swimming pool**.

**Bah! MY palace will have two swimming
pools, 100 computer rooms and 1,000
TV rooms.**

**Amsterdam, Holland**, has such swampy
soil that the Royal Palace had to be built on
**13,569** long **wooden poles** that were driven
into the ground.

The **Royal Palace** in **Laos** was built right on the river so that visitors could **hop off their boats** and straight into the palace.

# MAD
# MONARCHS

When **Catherine the Great** of Russia (1762–1796) discovered that she had **dandruff**, she **imprisoned her hairdresser** in an iron cage for three years so that no one would find out.

In August 1453, **Henry VI** of England lost his memory. For over a year, he just sat still without speaking.

**Queen Maria Eleonora** of Sweden (1620–1632) was so upset about the **death** of her husband King Gustavus Adolphus that she slept with his **heart hanging over her bed** in a golden casket.

**King Henry Christophe** of Haiti (1811-1820) decided to test his guards' loyalty by ordering them to **march over a cliff**. If they obeyed, they fell to their deaths. If they refused, Henry had them **tortured** and **executed**.

**King Charles VI** of France (1380-1422) was convinced he was **made of glass**. He didn't like travelling in case the movement of the coach shattered him.

**Charles VI** also wandered around his palace **howling like a wolf**. The queen used a **lookalike** to take her place in the king's bedroom because she was so fed up with him.

**George III** of England (1760–1820) became very ill later in his life and everybody thought he was **mad**. One day, he thought an oak tree was the **King of Prussia**. He got out of his carriage to talk to the tree and **shook hands** with one of its branches.

**Eric XIV** of Sweden (1560–1568) was a **mad dad**. His daughter made him so angry one day that he grabbed her hair and **ripped** it out by the roots.

**Frederick William I** of Prussia (1713–1740) had a special group of soldiers called the **Potsdam Giants**, who were **all very tall**. They weren't sent to battles – but if King Frederick was feeling miserable or ill, they marched through his bedroom to cheer him up.

**King Ferdinand I** of Austria (1835–1848) liked rolling around the palace, wedged in a **rubbish** basket.

**King Philip V** of Spain (1700–1746) sometimes behaved **very strangely** – he greeted important visitors wearing just his **nightshirt**, started trying to escape from the palace and even believed that he was a **frog**.

# BLOODTHIRSTY BEHEADINGS

**Emperor Yizong** of China (860–874) employed **twenty doctors** to cure his sick daughter. When they failed, the Emperor had them all **beheaded**.

In 1587, **Elizabeth I** of England (1558–1603) signed the papers ordering the **execution** of Mary Queen of Scots. Elizabeth later changed her mind, but by then it was **too late** and Mary had already been beheaded. Oops!

When **King Peter the Great** of Russia (1682-1696) discovered that his **wife** had a **boyfriend**, he had the boyfriend's head chopped off and **placed in a jar** on his wife's bedside table.

**Henry VIII** of England (1509-1547) sentenced his second wife, Anne Boleyn, to death, but instead of using **an axe**, he ordered an **expert swordsman** from France to perform the beheading with a sword.

Then Henry went off and enjoyed a **game of tennis** while Anne was being beheaded.

When **Charles I** of England (1625-1649) was **beheaded** in front of a large crowd, he wore two shirts to keep warm so that he wouldn't shiver and look frightened.

After **Lady Jane Grey's** nine-day reign of England in 1553, the future Queen Mary I sentenced Jane and her husband, Lord Dudley, to death. Lord Dudley was **beheaded** first, and Lady Jane had to see his **dead body** on a cart, with his head wrapped in a cloth.

**Henry VIII** of England (1509–1547) believed that his fifth wife, **Catherine Howard**, had betrayed him with **two boyfriends**. He had one of them **beheaded** and the other one **hanged, drawn and quartered**.

**Catherine Howard** was also beheaded and on her way to the Tower of London, she had to pass London Bridge where her boyfriends' heads were **stuck on spikes**.

In 1793, following the **French Revolution**, **Louis XVI** of France was executed by the guillotine in **Revolution Square**. His wife Marie Antoinette was **beheaded** nine months later.

**King Hardicanute**, King of Denmark (1035–1042) and King of England (1040–1042) hated his half-brother Harold Harefoot so much for **murdering** his other half-brother that he ripped open Harold's grave, had him beheaded and **threw his body into a bog**.

# MURKY
# MURDERS

In 1478, **Edward IV** of England (1461–1483) had his brother George **drowned** in a **barrel of wine** for plotting against him.

**Crown Prince Sado** (born 1735–1762) was the heir to the Korean throne. But Sado was always **killing people**, so his father ordered his soldiers to seal Sado alive in a **chest full of rice**.

**King Edward II** of England (1307–1327) was **imprisoned** in a well by his wife, Isabella of France, then **murdered** by a group of Isabella's men. They **suffocated** him with a cushion and stabbed him up the bottom with a **red-hot poker**. Ouch!

**Emperor Caligula** of Rome (37–41) was **attacked** and **stabbed** to death in an underground passage by a group of his own officers.

**Mary Queen of Scots'** husband was so **jealous** of her friendship with her servant that he ordered him to be **murdered in front of Mary** during a dinner party.

**Henry II** of England (1154–1189) and **Thomas Becket**, the Archbishop of Canterbury, were best friends, but when they had an argument Henry ordered four knights to **hack Thomas to death**.

**Emperor Elagabulus** of Rome (218-222) was only **nineteen** when he was **murdered** by a group of soldiers. They dragged his body through the streets on a **hook** and stuffed it into a **sewer**.

**Oops. Maybe being emperor isn't such a great job after all.**

**Henry IV** of England (1399–1413) had only been on the throne for **three months** when a group of his enemies **rebelled** against him. They failed, and Henry had them killed and **cut into pieces**.

In 1605, the **Gunpowder Plot** was an attempt to blow up the House of Lords and kill **King James I**. The plot failed when one of King James's lords searched the cellars underneath Parliament on 5th November and discovered **Guy Fawkes** with lots of **barrels of gunpowder**.

**Richard III** (1483–1485) was **butchered to death** by one of his own men at the Battle of Bosworth. His clothes were ripped from his body, then was tied to a horse and taken to a church to be buried.

Between 1456 and 1476, **Vlad the Impaler** of Romania had over **20,000** of his enemies killed by sticking **stakes** through their bodies.

# FAMOUS
# PHRASES

**Marie Antoinette of France (1774–1792)** is famous for saying: "Let them eat cake!" when there was no bread for poor people in Paris.

Marie Antoinette's **last words** when she was beheaded, were, "I'm sorry, sir, I meant not to do it." She was apologising because she'd trodden on her executioner's foot.

**Elizabeth I of England (1558–1603):** "I have the body of a weak and feeble woman, but I have the heart and stomach of a king."

## George III of England (1760–1820):

"A traitor is everyone who does not agree with me."

## Frederick II of Prussia (1740–1786):

"A crown is merely a hat that lets the rain in."

## Queen Mary I of England (1553–1558):

"There's only one thing I never did and wish I had done: climbed over a fence."

## Queen Victoria of England (1837–1901):

"Everybody grows but me."

The little Queen was 1.5 metres at her tallest but shrunk as she got older to 1.4 metres, which is about the same as a ten-year-old girl today.

Queen Victoria is especially famous for saying: **"We are not amused"** when one of her lords told a **rude joke**.

**Henry IV of France (1589–1610)**: "Great eaters and great sleepers are incapable of anything else that is great."

**Edward VIII of England (1936–1936)**: "The thing that impresses me most about America is the way parents obey their children."

**What? I want to move to America immediately.**

**Queen Louise of Sweden** when she first became queen in 1950 said: "People look at me as if I were something special. Surely I do not look differently today from how I looked yesterday!"

**King Henry the Horrible: "Out of my way, worm!"**

# MYTH AND MYSTERY

The King's men claimed that **Canute of England** (1018-1035) had **power over the sea**. But when the King sat on his throne on the beach and ordered the tide to go back, it didn't – and Canute got **wet feet**!

**Richard III** of England (1483-1485) is famous because people think he **murdered** his two young nephews – Edward, the true heir to the throne, and his little brother Richard. The boys were locked in the **Tower of London**, and disappeared in 1483. No one knows what really happened.

**If they were anything like Peter, who could blame him?**

**Robert the Bruce**, King of Scotland (1306–1329) hid in a cave after he'd lost a battle. He watched a **spider** try again and again to spin a web until it finally succeeded and it **inspired** him to keep fighting.

When **Mary Queen of Scots** (1542–1567) was executed, she hid her **pet dog** under her skirt. It was said that the dog missed its mistress so much it never ate again and died of **misery**.

A story was spread by her enemies that **Anne Boleyn**, one of Henry VIII's wives, had an **extra finger** which was supposed to prove she was a **witch**.

In 1216, it's said that **King John** was taking a short cut home when he lost **all his treasure** in quicksands.

**Henry I** of England (1100–1135) imprisoned his brother Robert because they were enemies. When Robert tried to escape, people said Henry had Robert's **eyes burned out** to prevent him getting away again.

According to **legend**, when **William the Conqueror** from France, invaded England, King Harold was killed at the Battle of Hastings in 1066 by an **arrow** in his eye.

The story of **Robin Hood** dates from the reign of **King Richard the Lionheart** (1189–1199). While Richard was away in France **fighting battles**, his brother John, was left to rule England. John made the poor people pay loads of taxes, so Robin Hood **stole** from the **rich** to give money back to the **poor**.

**If I'd been Robin Hood I'd have stolen from the rich and given to ME!**

**Tsar Nicholas II** of Russia (1894–1917), his wife and his five children were arrested during the **Russian Revolution**. The revolutionaries shot the entire family. Legend has it that one of the daughters, **Anastasia**, survived, and at least ten women have come forward **pretending** to be the **princess**.

# TOP
# TRENDS

**Queen Victoria** of England (1837–1901) was the first person to get married in a **white wedding dress.** It set a trend – before that, brides usually just wore their best dress.

**Richard II** of England (1377–1399) had a good idea. He used small pieces of cloth to keep his nose clean – in fact, he invented the **handkerchief**.

**Charles II** of England (1660–1685) had a long mane of curly black hair. This made **wigs** so **fashionable**, that wig makers took to snatching poor children off the streets and **shaving their heads** to make sure they had enough hair!

After **King Amanullah** of Afghanistan (1919–1929) stayed in London in 1927, he liked the fashion so much that he tried to make the men in his country wear **bowler hats**.

When **Henry VIII** of England got **older** and **fatter**, he wore padded clothes with puffy sleeves to hide his figure – and all the rich nobleman at court copied him.

**Louis XIV** of France (1643-1715) wasn't very tall so he wore a high **wig** and shoes with **high red heels**. The hair and heels became a trend, but Louis made it a law that **only the king** could wear red heels.

As **Edward VII** of England (1901–1910) grew fatter, he started leaving the bottom button of his waistcoat undone – and this quickly became popular among fashionable men.

**Queen Alexandra**, the wife of Edward VII walked with a **limp**. Fashionable ladies copied her and the walk was called the **Alexandra Glide**.

When **Peter the Great** of Russia (1682–1696) put a **tax** on men's beards, he unwittingly started a fashion for **false beards**.

**I'd put a tax on younger brothers.**

When **Henry I** of England (1100–1135) had his **hair cut**, all the men in the palace had theirs chopped off too. Then they trampled on the hair on the floor to prove their **hatred** of long hair and their **loyalty** to the king.

# ROYAL
# RECORDS

The **longest reigning** king ever was **Sobhuza II King of Swaziland** (1899-1982) who reigned for 82 years 254 days.

The **longest reigning British queen** was **Queen Victoria** (1837-1901) who reigned England for 63 years and 216 days.

The **shortest reigning** king ever was **King Louis XIX** of France who reigned for about 20 minutes on 2nd August 1830. The people of France had forced his unpopular father Charles X to give up the throne and they didn't want his son either.

The world's **heaviest** king was **King Tupou IV** of Tonga (1965–2006) who weighed 209 kilogrammes and had a 142 cm chest. He was so heavy that he had to have **special chairs** made for him!

The **tallest** ever king was **Peter the Great**, Emperor of Russia (1682–1696) who was two metres tall – about as high as a door!

The **richest** king in the world is the current King of Thailand, **Bhumibol Adulyadej**, who is worth about **£19 billion**.

**Hmm. Wonder if he needs an heir.**

The **largest palace and grounds** in the world is the **Palace of Versailles** in Paris. It covers a total area of **8,150,265** square metres – you could fit **2,000 football pitches** in the same space!

The **oldest ever** royal was **Princess Alice**, Duchess of Gloucester, who died in 2004 aged 102 years 308 days.

The **youngest** king alive today is **King Oyo**, the nineteen-year-old ruler of Toro, in Uganda, East Africa. He became king at the age of just **three**.

The **oldest** king alive today is **Abdullah bin Abdulaziz Al-Saud**, the King of Saudi Arabia, born in 1924. He's **even older** than the kingdom of Saudia Arabia itself, which wasn't formed until 1932.

The **most famous** royal jewels are England's **Crown Jewels**, worth nearly £15 million. The most expensive is the Crown, which was made for King George VI – it's decorated with five rubies, 11 emeralds, 17 sapphires, 273 pearls and 2,868 diamonds.

The **most expensive** crown in the world is Catherine the Great of Russia's **Imperial Crown**. Made of gold and silver, the crown is decorated with **5,000** diamonds.

# STRANGE
# BUT TRUE

**Ranavalona I** of Madagascar (1828–1861) became queen when her husband King Ramada **cut his own throat** and died. Queen Ranavalona had a secret ceremony where she was smeared with **bull's blood**.

Chinese **Emperor Shih Huang Ti** (247–221 BC) built 270 palaces all connected by **secret underground tunnels.** He was so terrified of being **murdered** that he slept in a different palace every night.

**Henry V** of England (1413-1422) led his army to victory at the **Battle of Agincourt**, where they succeeded in defeating a French army **more than three times** their size.

**Hatshepsut**, Pharaoh of Egypt (1473-1458 BC) was a **powerful woman** and a great ruler, but sometimes she had to strap a **false beard** to her chin and dress as a man to stay in power, because men were given more respect.

In the ninth century, there were **wolves** all over Wales. To get rid of them, **King Hywel Dda** made Prince Owain give him **300** wolves' heads every year.

**Queen Matilda** of England (April-November 1141) was **trapped** in Oxford Castle by her enemies. She was lowered from the castle on a **rope** by a few of the castle knights and escaped over the snow-covered fields camouflaged in a white cloak.

**Queen Elizabeth II** (1952-present) isn't allowed to go in the **House of Commons**. The last monarch to enter was King Charles I in 1642, when he attempted to **arrest** five members of parliament by force. Since then kings and queens have been **banned** from the House.

Any **whale** or **dolphin** found dead or alive within three miles of the UK shores belongs to the **king** and **queen**. The head of a dead whale belongs to the king, the tail belongs to the queen. This law is from 1317 when the queen needed whale bones for her **corsets**.

**Queen Elizabeth II** of England has **two birthdays**. Her **real** birthday is on 21st April. Her **public** birthday is celebrated early in June because the weather is usually better.

**Prince Charles** and **Prince William** of England never fly on the same **aeroplane**. They're the next in line for the throne and if they were both killed, William's younger brother Harry would have to be king instead.

At Edinburgh Castle, **King James IV** of Scotland (1488–1513) used to spy on his enemies in the Great Hall through a **small secret window** near the fireplace, called the Laird's Lugs, meaning **lord's ears**.

**King Al-Mutamid** (1069–1091) of Spain's wife had never seen **snow.** The King planted a hillside with almond trees so that the falling petals would cover the hillside in white, just like **snowflakes.**

In 1911 **George VI** of England (1936–1952) was **bottom of his class** in the final exams at the Royal Naval College. But because he was going to be king, everyone pretended he'd passed them anyway!

**King Edward VI** of England (1547–1553) was **naughty** at school, but his teachers weren't allowed to **punish** him. So another boy had to take the **beatings** in his place while Edward watched.

After Queen Victoria's husband **Albert** died, the Queen of England wore **black** for the rest of her life, and didn't appear in public for over **20 years**.

# DREADFUL
# DEATHS

**King Henry I** of England (1100–1135) died from **food poisoning** after eating too many lampreys (which are little eels).

**He should have stuck to chocolate.**

**King Albert I** of Belgium (1909–1934) died alone in the **mountains**. He fell when he was **rock climbing** and nobody found him for **nine hours**.

**William III** of England (1689–1702) was out riding when his horse **stumbled** on a **molehill**. William fell from his horse and **died**.

**King Alexander I** of Greece (1917–1920)
was bitten by his **pet monkey** and died from
**blood poisoning**.

When **Alexander III** of Scotland (1249–1286)
was **galloping** home in the dark to celebrate
his wife's birthday, his horse slipped and the
king fell and **broke his neck**.

When **Cleopatra VII** (51–30 BC), Queen of Egypt heard that her friend **Mark Anthony** had died, she made a **poisonous snake** give her a fatal **bite**.

**Ivan the Terrible** of Russia (1533–1584) was a **fierce** and **cruel** leader, but he died quietly **playing chess**!

**Bela I** of Hungary (1060–1063) died when the **canopy** over his throne **collapsed** on top of him.

**King John** of England (1199–1216) died of a **fever** and dreadful **diarrhoea** in 1216 after eating a meal of **peaches and cider**.

**See? Fruit IS poisonous.**

**George II** of England (1727–1760) had a fit when he was on the **toilet.** He **fell off** and died.

**King Adolf** of Sweden (1751–1771) died after eating a meal of lobster, caviar, kippers and champagne, plus 14 servings of his favourite pudding.

**George I** (1714–1727) died of a **heart attack** caused by terrible **diarrhoea** after he ate too many **strawberries**.

**Killer fruit again!**

**Eric XIV** of Sweden (1560–1568) started beheading people if they annoyed him. His brother John threw him in **prison**, and gave the prison guards permission to **poison him**. His last meal was a bowl of **pea soup** poisoned with **arsenic.**

**Avoid veg!**

**Henry VIII** was away in France when the English army beat the Scottish army at the battle of Flodden Field in 1513. Henry's wife, Catherine of Aragon, sent Henry the **blood-stained coat** of the dead Scottish king, James IV.

In 1303, the **Keeper of the Palace of Westminster** and **50 monks** tunnelled into Westminster Abbey to steal King Edward I's **Crown Jewels**. The Keeper was caught and hanged for the crime – and **his skin was stretched** across the treasury door as a warning to others. The monks got away with it.

When **King George I** of England (1714–1727) discovered his wife Dorothea had a **boyfriend** – the handsome Count Konigsmark – George sent the Count away and kept Dorothea prisoner in the palace for **32 years**. Many years later, when the palace was rebuilt, **the Count's skeleton** was found under the floorboards of Dorothea's dressing room.

# Bye!

# HORRID HENRY BOOKS

Visit Horrid Henry's website at **www.horridhenry.co.uk**
for competitions, games, downloads and a monthly newsletter.

# the
# orion star

Sign up for **the orion star**
newsletter to get inside information
about your favourite children's authors
as well as exclusive competitions and
early reading copy giveaways.

**www.orionbooks.co.uk/newsletters**

Follow  on

Orion
Children's Books